Transport

Aeroplanes

by Mari Schuh

a Capstone company — publishers for children

Raintree is an imprint of Capstone Global Library Limited, a company incorporated in England and Wales having its registered office at 264 Banbury Road, Oxford, OX2 7DY – Registered company number: 6695582

www.raintree.co.uk
myorders@raintree.co.uk

Edited by Carrie Braulick Sheely
Designed by Lori Bye
Picture research by Wanda Winch
Production by Katy LaVigne
Originated by Capstone Global Library Limited
Printed and bound in China

ISBN 978 1 4747 4434 8
21 20 19 18 17
10 9 8 7 6 5 4 3 2 1

British Library Cataloguing in Publication Data
A full catalogue record for this book is available from the British Library.

Acknowledgements
We would like to thank the following for permission to reproduce photographs: Alamy Stock Photo: SCPhotos, 13; iStockphoto: santirf, 20–21; NASA/Kennedy Space Center Photo Archive, 19; Shutterstock; Action Sports Photography, 15, Marcel Derweduwen, 9, MP_P, 11, T. Sumaetho, zoom motion design, tratong, 6–7, VanderWolf Images, 16–17, Volodymyr Kyrylyuk, 5; U.S. Air Force photo by TSgt Ben Bloker, cover

Contents

Up high

Look up in the sky!

An aeroplane

flies high.

Parts

Look at the jet engines?

They are loud.

They make this aeroplane move.

jet engine

A propeller spins fast.

It can move an aeroplane too.

See it go!

Aeroplanes have long wings.

They lift aeroplanes into the air.

Up they go!

Pilots fly an aeroplane.

They move levers.

They look at dials.

lever

Types

A crop duster flies low.

It is slow.

It sprays crops.

A fighter jet flies high.

It is fast.

It shoots at an enemy plane.

Cargo planes are full of goods.

They can carry post too.

Some can carry cars.

THE
AIRBUS INDUSTRIE

A jumbo jet flies far.

It carries many people.

Where will you fly?

A6-EOC

Glossary

cargo goods carried by an aircraft, ship or other vehicle

crop plants that farmers grow in large amounts, usually for food

dial face on a measuring instrument

enemy nation or army that is at war with another country

engine machine that makes the power needed to move something

fighter fast aeroplane with weapons that can destroy other aircraft

goods things that can be bought or sold

lever bar used to make a machine or vehicle work

pilot person who flies a jet or plane

propeller set of rotating blades that make the force to move an aeroplane through the air

Find out more

Books

Big Machines Fly! (Big Machines), Catherine Veitch (Raintree, 2015)

Look Inside an Airport (Usborne Look Inside), Rob Lloyd Jones (Usborne Publishing Ltd, 2013)

Machines at the Airport (Machines at Work), Sian Smith (Raintree, 2014)

Planes (Usborne Beginners), Fiona Patchett (Usborne Publishing Ltd, 2007)

Websites

www.dkfindout.com/uk/transport/history-aircraft/cargo-planes/
Learn about the history of cargo planes.

http://www.bbc.co.uk/education/clips/zpxw2hv
Discover how much fuel an aeroplane needs.

Comprehension questions

1. What parts of an aeroplane help it to fly?
2. What do different types of aeroplanes have in common?
3. How can aeroplanes help people?

Index